The
Rapture
and
the
End

Renus Cake
I Jn. 1:7

The Rapture and

What Will Happen to You?

the End

Renus Cabe

Pleasant Word (a division of WinePress Publishing, PO Box 428, Enumclaw, WA 98022) functions only as book publisher. As such, the ultimate design, content, editorial accuracy, and views expressed or implied in this work are those of the author.

All Scripture quotations, unless otherwise indicated, are taken from the *New King James Version*. Copyright © 1982 by Thomas Nelson, Inc. Used by permission. All rights reserved.

Scripture quotations marked NIV are taken from the *Holy Bible, New International Version®, NIV®*. Copyright © 1973, 1978, 1984 by Biblica, Inc.™ Used by permission of Zondervan. All rights reserved worldwide. WWW.ZONDERVAN.COM

Scripture references marked KJV are taken from the *King James Version* of the Bible.

Scripture references marked NEV are taken from *The New English Version*, © The Delegates of the United University 14655 and the Syndles of the Cambridge University Press 1961, 1978. Reprinted with permission.

Scripture references marked AMP are taken from *The Amplified Bible, Old Testament*, © 1965 and 1987 by The Zondervan Corporation, and from *The Amplified New Testament*, © 1954, 1958, 1987 by The Lockman Foundation. Used by permission.

Scripture quotations marked WEY are taken from *Weymouth: The Modern Speech New Testament* by Richard F. Weymouth, 2nd Edition (1903), Edited and Partly Revised by E. Hampden-Cooke.

Scripture references marked TEV are taken from *The Bible in Today's English (Good News Bible)*, © American Bible Society 1966, 1971, 1976. Used by permission.

Scripture references marked BAS are taken from *New Testament in Basic English* of the Bible

ISBN 13: 978-1-4141-1616-7
ISBN 10: 1-4141-1616-0
Library of Congress Catalog Card Number: 2009910371

This book is dedicated to my Lord and Savior,
the Lord Jesus Christ, who calls me His friend.
It is also dedicated to my wife, El Tora,
who is my next best friend and companion.

Contents

Introduction

ONE OF THE great fundamental truths of basic Christianity is that the Bible is the true Word of God. "All scripture is given by the inspiration of God" (2 Timothy 3:16). "Holy men of God spoke as they were moved by the Holy Spirit" (2 Peter 1:21). The Word of God is an eternal Word. "Heaven and earth will pass away, but my words shall by no means pass away" (Matthew 24:35).

The Bible is the sole basis for all teaching and doctrine. "If they do not speak according to this word, it is because there is no light in them" (Isaiah 8:20). Therefore, all teaching and doctrine has not only to be based upon God's Word, it also must agree with that Word. If any scripture is found that disagrees with, or contradicts the teaching, then the teaching is either in error, or else certain parts of the teaching are wrong.

There are several ways to establish teachings or doctrines. Study the Word of God to learn what it is saying and build upon that. Compare scripture with scripture to find out if there is any disagreement, for scripture must agree with scripture. It is line upon line, precept upon precept, etc.

Another way to establish teaching or doctrines is to take a certain scripture or scriptures and begin to build a teaching roughly based upon them. These are isolated scriptures that we can compare with other scriptures or other books in the Bible. When another portion of the Word disagrees with the teaching, the teaching is not correct. Some individuals twist and interpret Scripture so that it does not affect the teaching. In actuality, this process is taking a clear scripture and making it vague, and a vague scripture and making it clear. In this method, the doctrine rules over scripture. In the other method, scripture rules and guides the doctrine.

Quite a number of years ago *Reader's Digest* had this notation: "A lie, told 1,000 times, is easier to believe than the truth heard just once." This principle can also be applied to teachings and doctrines. In the church world, there are multitudes of different teachings and beliefs. What is one to believe? If a particular teaching is a very popular one, and through the years it is proclaimed in churches many thousands of times, it is easier to believe than one heard for the first time. Yet that seldom heard and unfamiliar teaching may be in line with the scriptures more than those that we have heard for years. It seems that in the attempt to make scripture agree with our teaching, we make clear scripture vague and vague scripture clear.

R. A. Torrey, then the superintendent of the Bible Institute, Chicago, (now Moody Bible Institute), wrote a textbook entitled, *What the Bible Teaches*. What a great title! That is exactly what we want to know. We don't need to know what this one or that one says about it, but what the Bible really says. We don't need to know what is popular, but that which is in agreement with Scripture. It is our purpose to bring what we believe and teach into agreement with the Scriptures.

It is great to be able to understand and comprehend things about the future, but it is also important to note this one thing, that our salvation is not based on our beliefs concerning eschatology. Rather, it is based upon our faith in the Lord Jesus Christ, on His redemption for us on the cross, and on the shedding of His redeeming blood for us. This is the one thing about which we must all be absolutely sure.

—Renus R. Cabe

CHAPTER 1

The Rapture

THE RAPTURE IS a favorite subject for many Christians today. Songs are written such as, "There's going to be a meeting in the air." We hear expressions such as, "If I don't see you again, I will meet you in the air." Actually, however, the word, "rapture," is not a Bible term. It is not found in Scripture. It comes from the account written by the apostle Paul in 1 Thessalonians 4:13-18.

> But I do not want you to be ignorant, brethren, concerning those who have fallen asleep, lest you sorrow as others who have no hope. For if we believe that Jesus died and rose again, even so God will bring with Him those who sleep in Jesus. For this we say to you by the word of the Lord, that we who are alive *and* remain until the coming of the Lord will by no means precede those who are asleep. For the Lord Himself will descend from heaven with a shout, with the voice of an archangel, and with the trumpet of God. And the dead in Christ will rise first. Then we who are alive *and* remain shall be caught up together with them in the clouds to meet the Lord in the

air. And thus we shall always be with the Lord. Therefore comfort one another with these words.

The Rapture, then, is the resurrection of those who have died believing and having faith in Christ. It also includes the believers who are alive at that time, who will join them as both groups are caught up in the clouds. There are many and varied teachings concerning this great event. Some believe it will happen before the time of the Great Tribulation. Some believe it will occur halfway through a seven-year tribulation, while others think that it will be after the tribulation. These teachings are usually known as, "Pre-tribulation, Mid-tribulation, and Post-tribulation." The most widely believed and preached is the Pre-tribulation theory. It is the one that we would like to examine more closely.

The Rapture, in this teaching, will take place prior to the Great Tribulation, which is, allegedly, a period of seven years. It is said to also correspond to the happenings told in Luke 17:34-36. Two men shall be sleeping in bed, one will be taken, the other one left. Two women will be grinding, one of them will be taken, the other left. Two men will be working in the field, one will be taken, the other left. This passage shows that the rapture could take place at any time or period, nighttime or daytime. There have been simulated newspapers printed telling of this event, huge headlines proclaiming, "THOUSANDS DISAPPEAR." Likewise simulated radio broadcasts have said the same thing. When the Rapture happens, it will be a time of great confusion in the world.

This teaching has been around for about 200 years and had its beginning in Ireland in the Plymouth Brethren Movement. This movement began in Dublin with a group of believers who met for prayer and fellowship. A man by the name of J. N. Darby became a member of the fellowship, and was prominent in the teaching of the pre-tribulation theory. The teaching also carried the name of "Darbyism." In the early nineteenth century, the post-tribulation theory was the main belief in America. Today, the pre-tribulation theory seems to be the prominent teaching in most denominations and churches concerning the second coming of the Lord. C. I. Scofield adopted this interpretation and used it in his many notes in the Scofield Bible, influencing many. The pre-tribulation theory was an unknown teaching before the rise of the Plymouth Brethren. But is it true? Is it accurate? Is it in agreement with Scripture? Does the Bible, as a whole, back it up? It is these questions we would like to examine.

The belief that Christ will appear in glory at the close of the Great Tribulation is something all agree with. But is there a secret coming before that? George E. Ladd, former professor at Fuller Theological Seminary, writes, "The natural assumption is that the rapture of the Church and the resurrection of the dead in Christ will take place at His glorious coming. The burden of proof rests on those who teach this is *not* the proper order of events."[1] Concerning Christ's teaching in Matthew 24, he again writes, "The Rapture of the Church before the Tribulation is an *assumption*; it is not taught in the Olivet Discourse."[2]

Some teach that when John was told in Revelation 4:1, "Come up here," this is the rapture of the church. That is a great misinterpretation. He was told, "Come up here [John], and I will show you things which take place after this." (See Chapter 2 in this book: "The Woman in Revelation 12.") John was being shown what was to happen in the future.

First, there cannot be a rapture without a resurrection. The dead in Christ will rise first, *and then* those that are alive and remaining will be caught up together with them. In Revelation 13:7 the beast (antichrist) will have authority over every tribe, tongue, and nation. That includes every

3

country, including the United States. Further, all who dwell on the earth will worship the beast, with the exception of those whose names are written in the Book of Life of the Lamb slain from the foundation of the world (vs. 8). An image is made and everyone is required to worship it, and if they do not, then they will be killed (vs. 15). Also, everyone is required to have a mark placed on their right hands or on their foreheads in order to buy or sell anything (vs. 16). Those that refuse all of this will be killed. They will become martyrs for the Lord.

In Revelation 20, the tribulation period is over and the Lord now takes over. Satan is cast into a bottomless pit where he will remain for 1,000 years. Verses four to six go on to read:

> Then I saw the souls of those who had been beheaded for their witness to Jesus and for the word of God, who had not worshipped the beast or his image, and had not received his mark on their foreheads or on their hands. And they lived and reigned with Christ for a thousand years. But the rest of the dead did not live again until the thousand years were finished. This is the first resurrection. Blessed and holy is he who has part in the first resurrection.

Because there cannot be a rapture without a resurrection, and the first resurrection is *after* the tribulation, that is when the Rapture will take place. Now we have a conflict. Do we make our teaching or our doctrine agree with Scripture, or do we make Scripture agree with our doctrine? Sad to say, adherents of this teaching have put the teaching first. Scripture has to be made to agree with the teaching. One of the first explanations given is that there have been a number of resurrections, even some at the time of the resurrection of Jesus. The most common explanation is that the first resurrection is in two parts: one-half before the tribulation, and the other half after the tribulation. In Bible College, a student asked the professor who was teaching the book of Revelation, "How could there be a pre-tribulation rapture if the first resurrection is after the tribulation?" The answer was, "The first resurrection is divided in two halves, one before and one after." Clarence Larkin also took this approach in his book, *Dispensational Truth*. This book was first copyrighted in 1918 and the revised edition was copyrighted in 1920. Larkin was great at drawing charts. The book is full of them. On one chart, he has the first resurrection in two parts, the first part before the tribulation is listed as, "First Resurrection Saints." The other half is listed as, "Tribulation Saints."[3]

There are three main references in the Bible concerning these future resurrections, one is spoken by Daniel, one is by Jesus, and the other is by the apostle Paul.

THE RESURRECTIONS

Daniel

And many of those who sleep in the dust of the earth shall awake, some to everlasting life, some to shame and everlasting contempt.

—Dan. 12:2

Jesus

Do not marvel at this; for the hour is coming in which all who are in the graves will hear His voice and come forth—those who have done good to the resurrection of life, and those who have done evil, to the resurrection of condemnation.

—John 5:28-29

Paul

I have hope in God, which they themselves also accept, that there will be a resurrection of the dead, both of the just and the unjust.

—Acts 24:15

In Revelation 20, we have a further explanation of these two resurrections. The thing that is different between these and other resurrections that have happened is that these are eternal resurrections. They are forever and forever. Whatever or wherever the future of the resurrected will be, it is for all eternity. The separation is made between those who have done good and those who have done evil, and between the just and the unjust. To one group it is to everlasting life, to the other everlasting contempt and condemnation. Nowhere is there any clue that either resurrection is to be divided into two parts, each part at different times. The only thing revealed in Revelation 20 is that the two resurrections do not happen at the same time. There is 1,000 years between the first and second resurrections. The first is before the thousand-year period (millennium); the second is after that period.

Another explanation to the two phases of the coming of the Lord (before and after the tribulation) is the two Greek words given to describe it. One is the word, *parousia*, which has the simple meaning of "coming." The other is the Greek word, *ephiphanae*, which has to do with brightness or manifestation. We are told that the first one is before the tribulation, and it is sort of a secret coming as far as the world is concerned. The other has to do with the events after the tribulation, in which the glory of the Lord will be revealed with great manifestation and brightness, and all will see Him.

All of this sounds quite plausible until we read the scripture found in 2 Thessalonians 2:8, "And then the lawless one will be revealed, whom the Lord will consume with the breath of His mouth and destroy with the brightness of His coming [the *parousia* of His *ephiphanae*]." So both Greek words are used for the same event or at the same time. There is *one* coming of the Lord. There is *one* first resurrection. And it all takes place at the end or after the tribulation period.

In his conclusion, George E. Ladd writes, "The scriptures which predict the Great Tribulation, the Rapture and the Resurrection, nowhere place the Rapture and the Resurrection of the saints at the beginning of the Tribulation. Nor does Scripture know anything of two phases of the first resurrection—that of the saints and that of the tribulation martyrs, separated by a seven-year tribulation. On the contrary, the one passage which is most specific as to chronology places the resurrection of both martyrs and saints after the Tribulation."[4]

The question arises, "What about those in Luke 17, where one is taken and the other left? And what about newspaper and radio broadcasts?" First, if the Rapture is after the tribulation (and I think we have proven that), there will be no newspapers printed, there will be no radio or TV broadcasts. There will be no tomorrow as far as the world is concerned. This will be the end of the current dispensation. So, then, the account in Luke 17 is not about the Rapture. What is it?

Most people quoting or talking about people being taken up—or out—stop short of the Bible account. In Luke 17:37 the disciples asked Jesus a question, "Where, Lord?" Where did they go, what happened to them? Jesus gave them a clue, although His answer was in the form of a riddle. "Wherever the body is, there the eagles will be gathered together."

Another question arises, "Does the church have to go through the tribulation?" This is a good question, and the answer is that some believers will, but others will not. The explanation is found in Revelation 12. Let's take a look.

CHAPTER 2

The Woman in Revelation 12

REVELATION CHAPTER 12 introduces us to this woman. Who is she? Some have suggested that she is Israel, others that it is Mary and it has to do with the birth of Christ. First of all, Mary was not caught away for three-and-a-half years. Second, Jesus was not caught up into heaven immediately after His birth. Some have suggested that the woman represents Jewish Christians. As far as God is concerned, there are no Jewish Christians. According to the Word of God, "There is neither Jew nor Greek, there is neither slave nor free, there is neither male nor female; for you are all one in Christ Jesus" (Gal. 3:28). If a Jew, or anyone else, is a born again Christian, they are part of the body of Christ. We may use terms like Jewish Christians (etc) as a means of identity, but God just recognizes each as simply Christians. One of the keys to the book of Revelation is found in chapter 4, verse 1 where John was told, "Come up here, and I will show you things which must take place after this." The King James Bible renders it, "Things which must be hereafter." Other translations:

NIV: "What must take place after this."
AMP: "What must take place in the future."
BAS: "Things which are to come."
WEY: "Which are to happen in the future."
TEV: "What must happen after this." (This also is used in *Good News for Modern Man.*)
NEV: "What must happen hereafter."

John was on the island of Patmos and the time was approximately in the years of the early 90s. That would be some 90 years after the birth of Christ and some 60 years after His crucifixion. What is to follow, then, was to be after that time period, or in other words, in the future. All that follows the word given to John in the book of Revelation is future. It is not past history. We believe that this is the end time church portrayed here—the Bride of Christ—to be revealed in the last days.

She is clothed with the sun, the moon is under her feet, and she is crowned with 12 stars. In Romans 1:20, Paul writes, "For since the creation of the world His invisible attributes are clearly seen, being understood by the things that are made, even His eternal power and Godhead . . . " So from creation we are able to have an understanding of the Godhead, the Father, the Son, and the Holy Spirit—a triune God. In all of creation, nothing does this any better than the sun, moon, and stars.

The sun is a symbol of the Father, the Father of Lights (see James 1:17). The moon reflects the light (or the glory) of the sun, the Son of God reflects the glory of the Father. The moon will be turned to blood (Joel 2:31), the sign of the Savior. The moon is under the woman's feet, her firm foundation. The stars represent the Holy Spirit. Abraham was to have seed as numberless as the sands on the seashore (earthly), and the stars in the sky (spiritual). This woman, then, is clothed in all the glory of the triune God. Paul's prayer in Ephesians 3:20,21, was that we might be filled with all the fullness of God. This woman has attained that. Again in Ephesians 5:27, "That He might present to Himself a glorious church, not having spot or wrinkle or any such thing, but that she should be holy and without blemish." This is that church.

Another sign appears—a fiery red dragon who is opposed to the woman (the church or bride). He persecutes the woman (see Revelation 12:13-16), but the woman is given two wings of a great eagle, and she flies into the wilderness where she is nourished for a time and times and half a time. In verse six, she is fed for 1,260 days, or three-and-one-half years—the period of the tribulation.

This answers the question of the disciples, "Where, Lord." His answer, "Where the body is, the eagles will be gathered."

Also a child is born. To quote Kevin Conner, "The man-child is the ultimate revelation of 'the seed of the woman' promised in Genesis 3:15, who would crush the serpent's head."[1]

W.W. Patterson writes, "The man-child is born as a result of the marriage of Christ and the church. A creation that is free from every taint of sin and corruption, begotten of a perfect father and born of a perfected mother."[2]

There is a number that do not go out with the woman into the wilderness. The devil, after he fails to catch the woman, goes after these people. In Revelation 12, they are called "the remnant of her seed" (KJV), or the "rest of her offspring." In verse 17 they are described as those who, "Keep the commandments of God and have the testimony of Jesus Christ." They are Christians, and as a remnant of the woman, they are another proof that the woman is Christian.

When one goes to a remnant sale and buys a piece of material, it is the very same material as the original bolt was. Why do these Christian believers miss the taking out of the church? They are the unwise virgin group seen in Matthew 25:1-13. They are the ones who do not have the wedding garment in Matthew 22:11-14.

THE TEN VIRGINS

Similarities of the virgins

> For I am jealous for you with godly jealousy, for I have betrothed you to one husband, that I may present you as a chaste virgin unto Christ.
>
> —2 Corinthiuans 11:2

1. They are all virgins.
2. They all had lamps.
3. They all had oil in their lamps.
4. All had their lamps burning.
5. They all slumbered and slept.
6. They all heard the midnight cry, "The Bridegroom is coming."
7. They all awoke and began to trim their lamps.

Differences of the virgins

Then what made the difference? The wise had an extra vessel with oil in it, while the foolish did not. When they all awoke and began to trim their lamps, the foolish discovered that their lamps were going out. The wise could not spare any of their oil, so while the foolish went to get oil, the Bridegroom came, and the door was shut. So, what made the difference? Oil!

G. Campbell Morgan, in his book, *The Parables and Metaphors of Our Lord*, writes, "Through the Old Testament oil is ever the symbol of the Holy Spirit. Whether in the lamp burning in the Holy Place, or whether in symbolism of such a one as Zechariah; whether in all those anointings of the ancient ritual, the oil was always typical of the Spirit and power. Our Lord surely used this whole parable in that connection, and for that purpose."[3]

The foolish virgins become the martyrs who have their names written in the Lamb's Book of Life, and who refuse to take the mark of the beast, or worship his image. All others during this period of time will receive the mark and the number of the beast. They will worship his image, thereby sealing their doom.

REVIEW

To review at this point, we have the emergence and revelation of the antichrist, the catching away of the church, the bride of Christ, going into a place where she is fed by the Lord for three-and-one-half years. She is not caught up, but she is caught *out*. The remnant of her seed goes into the tribulation period, where they will face great persecution and will eventually lose their lives. They will become martyrs for their testimony of Christ. In which of these two groups will each of us be found? Great changes are coming, some are bad and terrible things, some are good and blessed. A lot has to happen to bring the church (believers) to the place of the woman in Revelation 12. A last day revival is certainly a part of bringing her to that place of perfection.

CHAPTER 3

Revival

R *EVIVAL*. WHAT IS revival? For years we have made arrangements for special meetings, called in an evangelist, and put up a sign announcing, "Revival Meeting." Perhaps some people are actually saved during an evangelistic outreach, and that is a wonderful thing. But is it really revival?

Revival comes from the word, "revive," which has the meaning of restoration of life. If someone faints or passes out, we try to revive them, perhaps by artificial respiration. We bring them back to consciousness. If they are rescued from drowning, the same process is used to revive them. Revival is a restoration to spiritual life of those who have become faint or dull in their spiritual life.

Revival has to do mainly with the church, the people of God, who have become lukewarm or even cold in their spiritual lives. Charles Finney said that, "Revival is nothing else than a new beginning of obedience to God." And again, "Christians will have their faith renewed."[1] David explained it this way, "Restore unto me the joy of your salvation, and uphold me by your generous Spirit. *Then I will teach transgressors your ways, and sinners shall be converted to You*" (Psalm 51:12, 13). Again, Finney writes, "A revival always includes conviction of sin on the part of the church." Also, "Backslidden Christians will be brought to repentance."[2] When the church is revived, sinners will be saved. On the other hand, we can have an evangelistic crusade and sinners can be saved, but church members may not necessarily be revived.

In Psalm 85 we have a number of things that speak to us of revival. In verse 1, captivity is brought back. In verse 2, iniquities are forgiven. In verse 4, wrath and anger are taken away, and restoration is prayed for. What do we need? The writer of the psalm said we need "revival." "Will you not revive us again, that your people may rejoice in you?" (vs. 6).

We have discussed events that occur in the last days of this dispensation. Is there revival for the church as we approach the end of time? Although some do not agree, we believe there will be revival for the church. Those who do not believe, quote scriptures such as, "There will be a great falling away," and, "Because iniquity abounds the love of many will wax cold." And again, "He that endures to the end shall be saved." Given this viewpoint they say, "That doesn't sound like revival to me!"

We receive what we believe. Our faith must rest upon what God says—upon His promises. "Faith comes by hearing, and hearing by the word of God" (Romans 10:17). What we pray must be based upon the will of God. "Now this is the confidence we have in Him, that if we ask anything according to His will, He hears us. And if we know that He hears us, whatever we ask, we know that we have the petitions that we have asked of Him" (1 John 5:14-15).

Here are some basic examples of praying the will of God. We read many scriptures that have to do with salvation, and we know it's God's will to save sinners, so we can pray for the salvation of sinners with confidence. Likewise, scriptures about the Holy Spirit show us God desires us to be filled, so we can then pray for folks to receive the Holy Spirit. Healing involves the same principle, although some believe healing is not necessarily God's will. However, Mark 16:18 does not say, "They will lay hands on the sick, and they shall recover [*if it is the Lord's will*]." In James 5:14-15, it does not say, "Is anyone among you sick? Let him call for the elders of the church, and let them pray over him, anointing him with oil in the name of the Lord, and the prayer of faith will save the sick, and the Lord will raise him up [*if it be His will*]." We added the italics. These words are actually not in the Bible. We can pray in confidence that healing is His will.

So again the question, is there revival for the end time, before the Second Coming of Christ? To answer that question we turn to Acts 3:19-21:

> Repent therefore and be converted, that your sins may be blotted out, so that times of refreshing shall come from the presence of the Lord, and that He may send Jesus Christ, who was preached to you before, whom heaven must receive until the times of restoration of all things, which God has spoken by the mouth of all His holy prophets since the world began.

There are two thoughts or aspects of revival here, but first let us note the time element that is involved. It is the time of the second coming of Jesus. Where is He now? It says that He must be kept or remain in heaven. This was written *after* Pentecost. In Acts 1:9-11 we know how He went away. We also know that Stephen saw Him at the right hand of the majesty. And Jesus also told us that He is coming back again. Now we understand that He must "remain in heaven until . . . " (Acts 3:21). It is until a time of restoration of all things and a time of refreshing.

The first thought of revival in these verses is in the words "restore all things." Restore means: "To bring back into existence, use, or the like." "Reestablish." "To bring back to a former, original, or normal condition." "To give back, make return, or restitution." Restoration is the act of doing this. It speaks of "renewal, revival, and reestablishment."

Do we have an example of restoration in the Bible and the way in which God restores? Yes, in the book of Joel. In chapter one it says, "What the chewing locust left, the swarming locust has eaten; what the swarming locust left, the crawling locust has eaten; and what the crawling locust left, the consuming locust has eaten" (Joel 1:4). This verse prepares us for what is to follow in the book of Joel—a real time of disaster and heartache.

Because of these locusts, there were no vines or grapes, and because there were no grapes there was no wine. This resulted in a great cry of anguish from the alcoholics ("drunkards" in KJV). The locusts are described as a great army going forth, devouring everything in their path—the wheat, barley, and the fig, pomegranate, and apple trees. It was time to pray. This was a call to those who minister to lie in sackcloth and repentance. There was a call for a sacred assembly, a time of fasting and prayer. All were to be involved, including the children. The call went on to say, "Rend your heart, and not your garments. Return to the Lord your God, for He is gracious and merciful, slow to anger, and of great kindness. Who knows if He will turn and relent, and leave a blessing behind Him" (Joel 2:13).

What is the result? "I will restore to you the years the locust has eaten." (Joel 3:25a) Complete restoration!

Everything that was lost is now restored. A great example of how our God restores. Is all of this literal? Is it allegorical? Is it also eschatological? Probably all three are involved. Recorded in history are some terrible plagues of locusts that have taken place in the part of the world where Joel lived. But this passage reaches far beyond the literal, for there is, in Joel 2:28-29, the promise of Pentecost. There is judgment, but there is also restoration! Jesus must remain in heaven *until* a great restoration!

And now, in Acts 3, we see a restoration of everything that God has spoken through His prophets since the world began! Everything lost is restored! Everything the church has lost is restored. Restoration began with Martin Luther and the revelation of salvation as a work of grace. We have been in periods of restoration since then. Pentecost was restored to the church in the early 1900s. Now there is to be a complete restoration of all that the prophets have spoken since the world began. And then, Jesus comes! If that isn't revival, then what is it?

The second thought of revival at the end time found in these verses hinges on the words, "times of refreshing." When I was attending Bible College (late 1940s) the Weymouth translation that was being sold was in its fifth edition, and a man named Robertson had revised it. A Greek professor at the school told us that if we could find a first or second edition of Weymouth it would be a much better and more accurate translation. We found some used ones in England, and I have a second edition, printed in 1902. "Times of refreshing," is translated, "seasons of revival." Williams renders it, "times of recovery." The *Amplified Bible* has it, "times of refreshing, of recovering from effects of heat, of reviving with fresh air." The Greek word for these times of refreshing is *anapsuxis*, and this is the only time it is used in the New Testament. Strong renders it, "A recovery of breath, i.e. (fig.) revival."

A recovery of breath happens perhaps after fainting, or after having your breath knocked out. A runner, who loses his breath, gets what is called a "second wind," which takes him to the finish line. The church is getting close to the finish line, and revival, like a second wind, will take it to the end.

What do we learn from these verses? *Restoration*, and then Jesus returns. *Revival*, a recovery of breath, then Jesus comes back. Is there revival for the last days? The answer is a definite *yes!!* He must remain in heaven until these things are fulfilled.

Why revival? Surely the church today needs reviving, and if that reviving results in sinners being saved, it would be a marvelous thing. But this revival has more importance than just these things, wonderful as they are. Dean Sherman of YWAM (Youth with a Mission) asks this question, "What is God doing in the world today?" Then he answers the question, "He is building His church." We believe this is true, but He is building even more than a church, He is preparing a Bride. In our studies thus far, we have talked about Revelation 12 and about a woman clothed with the sun, her feet are on the moon, and she is crowned with 12 stars. We have shown that this is the bride of Christ, and she will be taken by eagles' wings into a place prepared for her by God, where she will be fed by the Lord for three-and-a-half years. A church filled with the fullness of God, without spot or wrinkle. Ask yourselves this question, "If it were today, would I be a part of this woman, and would I be taken out? Do I fit the description of the woman?" At the present time, most of us would surely be in the remnant group that does not go out with the woman. We must match all the requirements and descriptions of the woman (bride).

This time of restoration, of a recovery of breath, of revival, is to bring the church to that place the Lord wants her to be. We may not be there now, but God is working it all out. Before that time comes, many changes will take place. There will be fallings away, and the love of many will wax cold. Persecution for the church—for true believers—will increase. Divisions and separations will occur, people will either get in or else they will get out. Nominal Christianity will be a thing of the past. For Christians, it will either be a time of total separation or a time of going back to the world. A world government is coming, and this will be the last great revival for the church to get ready—ready for both the onslaught of the dragon, as seen in Revelation 12, and ready as the Bride to be taken out by the Lord to her place.

There are several scriptures in the New Testament that, in the *King James Version*, use the word "perfection," or "perfect." Among them are Hebrews 6:1 and 7:11. "Leaving the principles of the doctrine of Christ, let us go on unto perfection." Again, "If perfection were by the Levitical priesthood . . . what need was there for another."

Several Greek words, all related, are used in these scriptures, *teleloo, telelotes*, and *teleosis*. Strong interprets them, *teleloo*: "To complete, accomplish, consecrate, fulfill, make perfect." For the word, *teleotes*, "A completer or finisher." For the word *telelosis*, "Completion, perfection, performance." Many of the various newer translations of the Bible prefer to use, instead of perfection, the word maturity. "Let us go on to maturity." Why? This seems to make sense, for we all know that no one is perfect, and that we could never attain perfection in ourselves. Are we afraid of the word, "perfection"?

This perfection could never have taken place until the time of the end on earth, the time that we are now studying. The Bridegroom is a perfect being. The bride He takes will not be inferior to Him. She will be just like Him. As has been mentioned, God is not only building a church, He is building or preparing a bride. It is the ultimate in God's working. The woman in Revelation 12 is filled with the fullness of God. She is a perfect bride! The persecution that comes, the revival at the end time, and the working of the Holy Spirit, will bring this all about.

CHAPTER 4

The Marriage of the Lamb

THE MARRIAGE OF Christ to His bride is not often the subject of sermons. While it may be mentioned or referred to, it is not with much detail. Many believe we will meet the Lord in the air, and somewhere, somehow, there will be a wedding. It is, however, one of the most important subjects concerning the end time.

It is heaven being united with the earthly; deity united with the human. In Jeremiah 3:14, God says to Israel. "I am married to you." In Jeremiah 3:8, because Israel had gone after other gods, God said, "Then I saw for all the causes for which backsliding Israel had committed adultery, I had put her away and given her a certificate of divorce." (The only cause, by the way, that Jesus gave for divorce in Matthew 19.)

He told Israel, in Isaiah 62:4, that they would no longer be termed Forsaken or Desolate, but that they now would be called "Hephzibah, and their land Beulah." Beulah means "married," and Hephzibah, "My delight is in her." Then in verse five, "As the bridegroom rejoices over the bride, so shall your God rejoice over you." Here we have bridegroom and bride mentioned.

We read in the third chapter of John's Gospel about the disciples of John the Baptist coming to him with a complaint that many were coming to Jesus and were being baptized. John's answer was, "A man can receive nothing unless it has been given him from heaven. You yourselves bear me witness that I said, 'I am not the Christ,' but 'I have been sent before Him.' He who has the bride is the bridegroom" (John 3:27-29). John here identifies Jesus as the bridegroom, and His followers as the bride.

Then in Matthew 9:14-15, we see the disciples of John coming to Jesus with this question, "Why do we and the Pharisees fast often, but your disciples do not fast?" Part of Jesus' answer was, "Can the friends of the bridegroom mourn as long as the bridegroom is with them? But the days will come when the bridegroom will be taken away from them, then they will fast." Jesus now identifies Himself as the bridegroom.

Paul, in attempting to explain his concern for the Corinthians, asked them to bear with him in it all, for he was jealous for them with a godly jealousy. Then, "For I have betrothed (KJV 'espoused') you to one husband, that I may present you as a chaste virgin to Christ" (2 Cor. 11:2).

Finally, in Revelation 19:7-9, "Let us be glad and rejoice and give Him glory, for the marriage of the Lamb has come and His wife has made herself ready. And to her was granted to be arrayed in fine linen, clean and bright, for the fine linen is the righteous acts of the saints. Then He said to me, 'Write: blessed are those who are called to the marriage supper of the Lamb.'"

The scriptures used here are found in the Old Testament, the Gospels, the epistles, and the book of Revelation. Surely, the teaching of the marriage of the Lamb is not an isolated matter, but is very important to every believer. The marriage of the Lamb is scriptural, just like the warp and the woof of a fabric, this theme is woven into the Word of God.

THE MYSTERY OF CHRIST AND THE CHURCH, A MARRIAGE

In Ephesians 5:22-32 three things can be seen of Christ's relationship to the church:

1. Christ's REDEMPTION of the church. He is the head of the church and also her Savior (vs. 23). He gave Himself for the church (vs. 25), an act of love.

2. His PERFECTION of the church. Sanctified and cleansed by the washing of the Word (vs. 26). Note also John 15:3; 17:7; Ezekiel 36:25; Psalm 119:9; 1 Peter 1:22. It is a "Glorious Church." The root word is also used in Philippians 3:21; Colossians 1:11; Titus 2:13. She is spotless. Compare with the Song of Solomon 4:7 and 2 Peter 3:14. The word "spot" indicates a stain, defect, defilement, or disgrace. There are no wrinkles or "any such thing." She is holy, sacred, clean, innocent, modest, chaste, or pure. She is without blemish. The same Greek word is found in 1 Peter 1:19 and Ephesians 1:4. The church is faultless and without blame or blemish.

3. His MARRIAGE to the church. In this portion of Ephesians the apostle goes from the natural, or things concerning man and woman, to the spiritual, Christ and the church. Husbands love your wives as Christ loves the church. Husbands should love

their wives as their own bodies, just as the Lord does the church. For in marriage, a man should leave his father and mother and be joined to his wife, and the two become one flesh. Then, *this is a great mystery*, for Paul is speaking of Christ and the church!

The Bible has a number of things it calls mysteries. There is the mystery of iniquity, the mystery of godliness, and the mystery of faith. We have identified at least 16 of these mysteries. While all are important and intriguing and make interesting studies, the mystery of Christ and the church, the marriage of the Lamb, is the most important one of all of them. It is the climax of all that God has been doing since the creation of man.

In Leviticus 21:10-15 we have the requirements for the High Priest in choosing a bride. In Hebrews 7:26 and 8:1, Christ is identified as our High Priest. The High Priest could not just marry anyone; she first of all had to be a virgin. He could not marry a widow or a divorced woman. She could not be profane or a harlot. And she had to be a virgin of his own people.

Jesus, our high priest, also cannot take just any bride. She has to meet all the requirements. The woman in Revelation 12 does just that.

When does this wedding take place? This is part of the mystery. The general belief is that it will happen sometime, somewhere in heaven, although no scripture actually states that. In the story of the ten virgins in Matthew 12, the church is still unmarried. She is a virgin waiting for the Bridegroom. She has been espoused, or engaged, but is still waiting. Matthew chapters 24 and 25 were not given as public discourses, but were given to the disciples privately. These chapters tell of events that will be on earth in the end time. The woman in Revelation 12 is pregnant; she is already married, so the marriage has already taken place. Paul says that this is a *great* mystery.

What is the purpose of this marriage, actually any marriage? An old standard book used by ministers for various services is *The Star Book for Ministers*, published by the Judson Press. Part of one of the marriage ceremonies reads:

> Divine revelation has declared marriage to be honorable in all. It is an institution of God, ordained in man's innocency, before he had sinned against his Maker, and been yet banished from Paradise. It was given in wisdom and in kindness, to repress irregular affection, to support social order, and to provide that, through well-ordained families, truth and holiness might be transmitted from one age to another.[1]

It goes on to say more, but it has in it the thought or idea of families. When God created Eve (Genesis 2:18), He said, "It is not good that man should be alone; I will make a helper comparable to him." One purpose for marriage was for companionship. Our trouble often is that we stop short of the things God does or is doing. Many stop at salvation. After salvation, we fail to go on to the baptism of the Holy Spirit. Receiving the Holy Spirit, we then stop there, as though we had it all. Actually, there is no stopping place in our faith.

Another purpose of marriage is to produce children. The *Star Book's* ceremony mentions families. After the creation of man, God said, "In the image of God He created him; male and female He created them. Then God blessed them, and said to them, 'Be fruitful and multiply; fill the earth and subdue it'" (Gen. 1:27-28). After the flood, Noah was told by God, "As for you, be fruitful and multiply; Bring forth abundantly in the earth and multiply in it" (Genesis 9:7). In Genesis 35:10-11, God appears to Jacob, and Jacob's name is changed to Israel. Jacob was told to be fruitful and to multiply.

In discussing the use of the institution of marriage, from the *Bible Encyclopedia*, "The most characteristic use of marriage and the family by Our Lord, is that in which He describes the kingdom of God as a social order in which the relationship of men is like that of sons to a father, and their relation to each other like that between brothers."[2]

Again it is about reproduction, about family.

The question arises, "Is this literal, or is it spiritual? W. H. Offiler writes, "The marriage of the Lamb is as literal as it is spiritual, and vice-versa."[3] Again, "The Manchild is the divine human product of the marriage of the Lamb of God, Jesus, to the Church, Matthew 25:10."[4]

Spiritual, this most can understand, but literal? Many would say, "Oh, no, not literal." The reasons for not believing this is literal are much the same as the reasons some say they cannot accept the virgin birth. All types have their fulfillment in reality. This marriage cannot remain figurative forever. *It must end in reality!* Hindsight is so much easier than foresight. Yes, Paul, what a great mystery this is!

CHAPTER 5

Daniel's
Seventieth Week

THE 70 WEEK prophecy given in Daniel 9, is one of the most comprehensive prophesies in the Bible. It is far-reaching in time, starting from the rebuilding of Jerusalem after the Babylonian captivity, and reaching on to the end of the age. This prophecy is an interesting study all by itself. We, however, are most interested in the last, or seventieth, week of that prophecy. The interpretation of that portion has direct influence in our understanding of our subject and it is found in Daniel 9:24-27.

The 70 weeks are actually weeks of years, or 70 times seven, which equals 490 years. Sixty-nine weeks (or 483 years) will be the amount of time starting from the command to rebuild Jerusalem unto the coming of the Messiah. "Messiah" (Hebrew) and "Christ" (Greek) both mean the very same thing. They mean "The Anointed," or "Anointed One." Thus, after the coming of the Messiah, there are seven years remaining in the prophecy.

The most prevalent and popular teaching concerning this week is that at its beginning, the Antichrist appears, and he makes a covenant with the Jews. The Jews are now allowed to return once again to the offering of live sacrifices. In the middle of the week, or after three-and-a-half years, he breaks the covenant, which brings about great persecution and suffering. But is this teaching found in the prophecy? Let's look at the verses more carefully.

The reach of the 69 years was, "Unto Messiah," or the "Anointed One." When did that take place? It was at the River Jordan, when Jesus was baptized by John the Baptist, and the Holy Spirit came upon Him in the form of a dove. The Anointed One, then 30 years of age, began His public ministry. In Daniel 9:26 we read that, "Messiah shall be cut off, but not for Himself." The margin here says, "Shall have nothing." It is also translated this way in the *Amplified Bible*. Concerning Jesus, we read that foxes had holes, and birds had nests, but He had no place to lay His head. At His crucifixion, the only thing He actually owned was a seamless robe. When He began His public ministry, he was separated from His natural family—His mother and His brothers and sisters. "Not for Himself," is also true, for it was for us that He ministered and then gave us His life.

Where most people take the wrong turn is in interpreting Daniel 9:27. "He shall confirm the covenant with many for one week" (KJV). The popular teaching is that this is the Antichrist, and he will make a covenant with the Jews. In order to find out who the "he" is, we must go back to preceding scripture in order to find the antecedent of the word "he." In the previous verse (Daniel 9:26), the subject is people, "The people of the prince who is to come." "Of the prince who is to come" is a prepositional phrase describing who the people are, and is not the subject. One must go back to, "Messiah shall be cut off," to find the antecedent of the word "he."

"He [Messiah] will confirm the covenant." "Now I say that Jesus Christ has become a servant to the circumcision for the truth of God, to confirm the promises made to the fathers" (Romans 15:8 KJV). In His three-and-a-half years of ministry, Jesus was confirming the covenant made with the fathers. The King James Version has it correct, it is "the" covenant, and the devil cannot confirm God's covenant! In Job 41, we read of a creature called "Leviathan." Like the serpent and the dragon, this is a figure that represents the devil.

The questions asked in Job 41 all require the same answer, "No." For example, from the fourth verse, "Will he make a covenant with you?" The answer is, "No," (This same principle, where the expected answer is "No," is also seen in 1 Corinthians 12:29-30. "Are all apostles, are all prophets, etc.") To correctly interpret Daniel's prophecy it is essential to understand that it is Jesus confirming the covenant.

"In the middle of the week (or after three-and-a-half years), He shall bring an end to sacrifice and offering" (Daniel 9:27). When Jesus died on the cross He died to end all sacrifices, His was a perfect and complete sacrifice. Hebrews 7:26-27 says, "For such a high priest was fitting for us, who is holy, harmless, undefiled, separate from sinners, and has become higher than the heavens; who does not need daily, as those high priests, to offer up sacrifices, first for His own sins, and then for the people's, for this He did *once* for all when He offered up Himself." "By that we have been sanctified through the offering of the body of Jesus *once for all*." "But this Man, after He had offered one sacrifice for sins *forever*, sat down at the right hand of God." "For by *one offering* He has perfected forever those who are being sanctified" (Hebrews 10:10, 12, 14, emphasis mine.) Read

31

also Hebrews 10:1-7. Jesus died to end all sacrifices. His was the perfect sacrifice.

The first half of Daniel's seventieth week has therefore been fulfilled, which then leaves only three-and-a-half years. We never read of seven years concerning this period, only three and a half. In Daniel 7:25; 12:7, "Time, times, and half a time." In Revelation 12:6, "One thousand two hundred and sixty days;" 12:5, "Forty-two months;" In 12:14, "Time, times, and half a time;" 13:5, "Forty-Two months." These all equal three-and-a-half years—the period of time that remains of Daniel's seventieth week. It is the period of the coming Great Tribulation.

W.W. Patterson writes, "Christ's work of confirming the covenant for seven years finds its fulfillment in His three-and-a-half years of earthly ministry ending in His crucifixion, and will be completely fulfilled in the three-and-a-half years of the Great Tribulation through His two witnesses (His anointed ones—sons of oil) Moses and Elijah. (Revelation 11)"[1]

The prophecy of Daniel is a very complex prophecy. One should study the whole of Daniel chapter nine, for it also includes a number of things that will come to pass, some even before the revelation of the Antichrist. These are momentous days, and these things should not happen to the saints of God as a surprise. One of the purposes of these writings is to see from God's Word things that will take place at the end of the age so that we will not be taken by surprise.

CHAPTER 6

The Great
Tribulation

I N OUR STUDIES thus far, we have seen the persecution of the church in Revelation 12, and the dragon turning on the remnant of her seed. The dragon, of course, is a picture or symbol of the devil, just as the serpent is. The question arises: is this literally Satan, or is it one that he has inspired? Is it actually the antichrist? If it is, then he is revealed sometime before the three-and-a-half years, and there is a time of persecution prior to the woman going to her place.

The teachings for this period of time are mainly found in the books of Daniel and Revelation. Both reveal the coming of a world ruler, the antichrist. Various names are revealed concerning this person. Some of them are:

1. Antichrist. 1 John 2:18, 22.
2. The little horn. Daniel 8:9
3. That wicked. 2 Thessalonians 2:8. (NIV and AMP, "Lawless one.")

4. Man of sin. 2 Thessalonians 2:3
5. Beast. Revelation 13:1

Daniel gives a description of this man, along with some of his actions. In Daniel 12:9, Daniel is told that this will be revealed in the last days. In Daniel 11:30-32, this one coming will be against the holy covenant. In 11:36, he will do everything according to his own will. In Daniel 7:25; 11:36, he will exalt himself above every god, and will speak blasphemies against the God of gods. He will not regard the God of his fathers (Dan.11:37), which indicates there has been some involvement or exposure to the worship of God. He will magnify himself above God (Dan.11:36), and he will be involved with a strange god (Dan. 11:39).

He is the little horn revealed in Daniel 7:8, and he is a man who speaks great things (7:20). In 7:21 he will make war with the saints and will prevail against them. (The remnant of the woman's seed.) In 8:25 he will stand against the Prince of Peace, but in the end he will be broken.

Daniel wondered just when all of this would take place. When would it end? He was told that it would be for a "time, times and half a time." That is a period of three-and-a-half years. This leader will last until the Ancient of Days comes (the coming again of Christ), and the saints will possess the kingdom (Daniel 7:22). All of this is for the "time of the end" (Dan. 8:17). It will be at the end of the "indignation," (the tribulation period) the time appointed for the end. (8:19)

In the book of Revelation, we find more details concerning this being and his world rule. Up until now in history, we have had a number of dictators—men who ruled their country with an iron hand. Some were guilty of great persecution and killings—men like Hitler and the persecution and killing of the Jews. It goes all the way back to the intolerance of the Roman Empire and the persecution, arrest, and the killings of Christians. Those past dictatorships involved an empire or a country. Bad as those times were, they don't compare with that which is to come at the end of this age. This is not concerning just a country or an empire, but it is over the entire world. There never has been a time such as this time will be, and there never will be again.

What makes this period especially bad is that the devil will have been cast down to the earth (Rev. 12:10). He is called the "accuser of our brethren," which is especially shown in the case of Job as Satan appeared before God and made his accusations. But not any more! In Revelation 12:12 we are warned by God, "Woe to the inhabitants of the earth and the sea! For the devil has come down to you, having great wrath because he knows he has a short time." Actually, he has only three-and-a-half years to let loose his fury and rage. He will no longer appear before God making his accusations.

As shown in a previous chapter about the woman in Revelation 12, the dragon comes against this woman described as being clothed with the sun, her feet on the moon, and crowned with a diadem or garland of 12 stars. In Revelation 12:13, just as soon as the devil was cast down to the earth, he began to persecute the woman—the bride. But he fails here, for the woman is given two wings of a great eagle so that she might fly into the wilderness. She is kept there, and nourished by the Lord, for three-and-a-half years, the length of the great tribulation. After the dragon's failure, he now turns to the remnant of the woman's seed, those who did not go out with the woman, but they do have a testimony of Jesus Christ (Revelation 12:17).

Revelation 13 introduces us to the beast (a name or description of the antichrist), rising up from the sea. This is what John saw, but it is probably not literally out of the sea, but out of the sea of humanity. From the dragon, the devil, he is given power, a throne, and great authority. People begin to worship both the dragon and the beast, saying, "Who is able to make war with him?" (Rev. 13:4). As seen in Daniel, he is a great spokesman. He was given, "A mouth speaking great things and blasphemies" (Rev. 13: 5). He blasphemes God, His name, His tabernacle, and those who dwell in heaven. He makes war with the saints, actually the remnant of the woman's seed. He has the authority to rule over every tribe, every tongue (language), and every nation (Rev. 13:7). Everyone who dwells on the earth will worship this being, *except* those who have their names written in the Book of Life of the Lamb slain from the foundation of the world. Of course, these would be the remnant of the woman's seed. Some have said that when all of this happens, they would profess Christ at that time and become martyrs. Not so! At this time it will be too late.

In 1947, I heard a camp meeting speaker who related a strange experience. He was in New York City, and along with another Spirit-filled preacher, they decided to visit Father Divine's place of worship. This man had great power over the people, so much so, that his religion could have been classified as a cult. When they went into the place, Father Divine had not yet arrived. People were singing songs of worship—hymns that we sing to Christ, but they were singing them unto Father Divine. Soon he entered the hall and the people began to fall down before him and worship him. The two ministers felt a power that was trying to pull them down before this man. They said to one another, "Let's get out of this place!"

Father Divine was not the antichrist, but the spirit of the antichrist was upon him. If the power of this man was so great that it began to pull down two Spirit-filled preachers, what will the real power of the antichrist be? The remnant of the woman's seed has a testimony of Christ. Their names are written in the Lamb's Book of Life. They will not worship the beast, but all others will.

Another beast now enters the scene. He is a supporter of the first beast. He has all the power of the first beast, and he causes everyone in the world to worship the beast (Revelation 13:11-12). He is able to perform great signs and miracles, such as making fire come down from heaven (vs.13). An image is made of the beast, and this second beast or false prophet, causes breath to come to the image, and causes it to speak. Everyone is made to worship the image, and if they will not, they are killed (vs.15). Further, he causes everyone, small and great, rich and poor, free and slave, to receive a mark on either their right hand or their forehead. Without this mark, no one will be able to buy or sell. It is the number of the beast or antichrist, and his number is 666 (vs.16-18). Six is the number of man who was created on the sixth day. Six days were given for him to labor, the seventh day was a day of rest. Now the number is tripled, and it identifies the man of sin.

How long does this go on? "He was given authority to continue 42 months," or three-and-a-half years. The devil knows he has but a short time, so probably the Antichrist also knows the same thing. The three—the devil, the first beast (Antichrist), and the other beast or false prophet, knowing they have but a short time, will unleash all the powers of hell. There have been tribulations, but this is why it is called the Great Tribulation.

Paul, writing in 2 Thessalonians 2:1-5, says that the coming of the Lord will not happen until this man of sin is revealed. Here he is called the son of perdition, and he will exalt himself above all that is called God. He will sit in the temple of God, showing that he himself is God. This mystery of lawlessness is already working. Only One is restraining it or keeping it back. That One is the Spirit of God in the church, holding back the powers of hell (2 Thessalonians 2:6-8), until the woman, the bride, is taken out.

Paul describes the rule of this being, the lawless one, as coming with the working of Satan with all power, signs, lying wonders, and deceptions (2 Thessalonians 2:8-10). In describing some that will follow him, Paul writes that they shall perish, because, "They did not receive the love of the truth, that they might be saved. And for this reason God will send them strong delusion, that they should believe the lie, that they might be condemned who did not believe the truth but had pleasure in unrighteousness" (2 Thessalonians 2:11-12). This shows our responsibility to hear and obey the truth, and to hide the Word of God in our hearts. For there is a spirit coming that will seek to capture us.

In Chapter 1, concerning the Rapture, we saw that it comes at the end of the tribulation period. The Lord is described in 1 Thessalonians 4:16-18 as coming with a shout, with the voice of the archangel, and with the trumpet of God. A further description is found in Revelation 19. Here Jesus is shown coming on a white horse. He is called, "Faithful and True" and "His eyes were as a flame of fire" (Rev. 19:11-12). He is crowned with many crowns. He is clothed in a robe dipped in blood, and His name is called the Word of God.

The armies that are in heaven follow Him also on white horses, and out of His mouth there goes a sharp sword. The beast, along with the kings of the earth who are allied with him, attempt to make war against this One coming in clouds of glory. Thinking about this present day and its manner of warfare, they will be launching everything available against the One coming with the armies of heaven. That would undoubtedly include nuclear weapons. What must be their consternation when the smoke dissipates and Christ and His armies are still there! What happens to the rest of the people is described in the remainder of the chapter. The beast and the false prophet are cast into the lake of fire, 1,000 years ahead of others, while the devil is cast into a bottomless pit. This begins a new period, as far as time is concerned. Soon the keeping of time will be no more. The thousand years is the last measurement of time. Then eternity begins and time will be no more.

CHAPTER 7

The Millennium

FOLLOWING THE PERIOD of the Great Tribulation there is a period of 1,000 years commonly known as the millennium. It is a Sabbath, a holy time and place. God is a God of order and of pattern. He created the world in six days, and the seventh day He rested. He gave man six days to work, the seventh day was a day of rest, a Sabbath. Then He gives mankind 6,000 years (One day equals 1,000 years, 2 Peter 3:8). The seventh day, or 1,000 years, is a day of rest—a Sabbath.

There is a rest in salvation, in our coming to the Lord (Matthew 11:28). There is a rest in the yielding to the Holy Spirit (Isaiah 28:11-12). The writer of the book of Hebrews spoke of a number of rests. In chapter three, he speaks of the rest promised Israel when they went into the Promised Land (Hebrews 3:7-11). In Hebrews 4:8-9, "If Joshua had given them rest, then He would not have spoken later of another day." Earlier in verse four, this rest is identified with the seventh day; and in verse nine, "There remains a rest for the people of God." This, the millennium, is that rest.

WILL THERE BE SINNERS IN THE MILLENNIUM?

A common belief seems to be that when the Lord returns everything and everyone will just continue on as they are now. The church will rule and reign with Christ, and will take over the government. Some have said they want to be mayors or governors. It would seem that the rule is over ungodly sinners. Does this mean sinners have a second chance?

During the tribulation period, those who have had their names written in the Lamb's Book of Life will not worship the Antichrist or take his mark or number, and they will be killed. That leaves alive all the rest of the people, people who have worshipped and taken his mark. If there were sinners in the millennium, then it would have to be be these people. What does the Bible say about them? In Revelation 14: 9-11, we read, "Then a third angel followed them, saying with a loud voice, 'If anyone worships the beast and his image, and receives his mark on his forehead or his hand, he himself will also drink of the wine of the wrath of God, which is poured full strength into the cup of His indignation. He shall be tormented with fire and brimstone in the presence of holy angels and in the presence of the Lamb. And the smoke of their torment ascends forever and ever; and they have no rest day or night, who worship the beast and his image, and whoever receives the mark of his name.'"

In the late 1950s or early 1960s, we had a Seattle area fellowship made up of pastors from a number of denominations and independent churches. They were gathered for three days of reviewing eschatology. The main teacher was a man from England who went step by step through the various teachings, the purpose being to get everyone to agree with the teaching or doctrine. The moderator of the sessions was the president of a local Christian college. At the time this writer was an associate pastor who attended those sessions.

When they were in their discussions concerning the millennium and sinners being there, this writer questioned this teaching. Quoting from Revelation 13:8 that *"all"* whose names are not written in the Lamb's Book of Life will worship the Antichrist and will take his mark. I then went to chapter 14 to show what happens to them. The moderator made this statement, "Evidently, in this case, "all" doesn't mean "all," for some will avoid taking the mark or worshiping the beast!" I sat down quite dumbfounded and thought of various passages of Scripture, such as: "All that call on the Lord will be saved." Well, maybe not "all"! "All that come to Him He will in no wise cast out." But what about the times when all doesn't always mean all, will some be cast out and not received? Or, in 2 Corinthians 5:14-15, "Because we judge thus: that if One died for all, then all died. And He died for all." In the giving of the Great Commission, Jesus in Matthew 28:18 said, "All power is given unto me" (KJV). In the New King James Version, it is, "All authority." This authority (power) was given so that the disciples going out into the world would have assurance and support. If you change the meaning of a word in one scripture, then how can that word be trusted or believed in any scripture? The fact is that "all" really does mean "all"! It can be clearly seen, as noted, that serious damage can happen when we twist the meaning of a word or text. We just cannot change the meaning of words in order to maintain our doctrines and our teaching.

Also see what happens when the Lord returns. In 2 Thessalonians 1:7-10, "And to give you who are troubled rest with us when the Lord Jesus is revealed from heaven with His mighty angels, in flaming fire taking vengeance on those who do not know God, and on those who do not obey the gospel of our Lord Jesus Christ. These shall be punished with everlasting destruction from the presence of the Lord and from the glory of His power."

In 1 Corinthians 15:50, we read that, "Flesh and blood cannot inherit the kingdom of God; nor does corruption inherit incorruption." In other words, the natural man cannot enter the kingdom age—the millennium. "We shall all be changed, in a moment, in the twinkling of an eye, at the last trumpet. For the trumpet will sound, and the dead will be raised incorruptible, and we shall be changed" (vs. 51-52).

In the light of these scriptures, how can one possibly believe there are ungodly living in the millennium? Read all of 1 Corinthians 15 to get the whole picture. The devil himself, the accuser of the brethren, will not be around. He will have been cast into the bottomless pit, to remain there for the whole 1,000-year period.

Let's do a little reviewing. The only ones alive at the coming of the Lord will be those who have worshiped the Antichrist and the woman in Revelation 12 who has been kept and fed by the Lord. When the Lord comes, those who have worshiped the Antichrist will be slain as we have seen. That just leaves alive the woman in the wilderness. The dead in Christ will rise first, and those alive (the woman, the bride) will join them. These all go into the rest, the Sabbath, the kingdom age, and the millennium. Our friend, Kevin Conner from Australia, has entitled one of his books, "*The Christian Millennium.*" That is exactly what the millennium is about. It is for the believer, not the unbeliever. It will be both Old Testament saints and New Testament saints, those who have died in Christ, or died looking ahead to Christ. Some people have this question, "Then who are we going to rule over?" Just why are you so taken up with the idea of ruling or being over others? It will be a time of godliness, and Christ will be in charge, He will rule. Then where do we all fit in? Well, are all resurrections exactly alike? All those resurrected will be alike in having bodies that will be immortal, and will also be incorruptible. There are also differences in the resurrection, as Paul writes in 1 Corinthians 15:40-42, "The glory of the celestial is one, and the glory of the terrestrial is another. There is one glory of the sun, another glory of the moon, and another glory of the stars; for one star differs from another star in glory. So also is the resurrection of the dead." God does all things well, and whatever our state or position is to be in the resurrection, it will be very acceptable, for in this kingdom there is no sin, no sickness, no devil, and no jealousy. None of these fleshly things will be there. In the parable of the giving of money to invest (see Luke 19:12-27) the one that gained the most (ten minas) was given rule over ten cities. Does that mean he would rule over ten cities in the millennium? I don't think so. It was a parable given to teach us certain lessons. I learned early on a saying, "Don't make a metaphor run on all fours!" The lesson here is that we will be rewarded according to our faithfulness in the measure that God has blessed us. God will always do everything right, and no one will be disappointed.

Our bodies will be much different than our present ones. Paul writes that we shall be changed, in a moment, in the twinkling of an eye, at the last trumpet. The dead in Christ are raised incorruptible, and those who remain shall be changed into the same state. These people will be immortal (see 1 Corinthians 15:50-54). What will that immortal glorified body be like? We really don't fully know, but what we do know is that, "We shall be like Him [Jesus] for we shall see Him as He is" (1 John 3:2). Our minds and our thinking will be so much different than they are today.

There will be no carnal thinking. It will truly be a time of peace on earth, ruled by the Prince of Peace Himself.

At the end of the thousand years, things change drastically. The devil is released from the pit or abyss where he has been bound. This hasn't changed him at all. He is still the great deceiver. As seen previously, the second resurrection does not occur until the thousand years are complete (see Rev. 20:5-6). It is now time for the second resurrection to take place. In Revelation 20:7-10, Satan goes out to deceive those that are in [not on] the face of the earth. These go up on the breadth of the earth. They are *in* the earth, and they go *up* onto the breadth of the earth. They have been in the grave, but they are now resurrected. Under Satan's leadership, they surround the saints as they go to war. It isn't much of a battle, for fire comes down out of heaven and destroys them. Satan is cast into the lake of fire and brimstone where the beast and the false prophet have been for a thousand years.

The next thing to take place is the white throne judgment. Anyone not found written in the Book of Life will be cast into the lake of fire, which is called the second death. Death and hell (hades) will also be cast into the lake of fire (see Rev. 20:13-15). Following this there is a new heaven and a new earth, the first heaven and the first (or present) earth will have passed away. This future and eternal place is described in Revelation 21 and 22. Eternity begins and time will no more. Today we live by the light, the energy and the power of the sun. Then, according to Revelation 21:23, "The city had [has] no need of the sun or of the moon to shine in it, for the glory of God illuminated [illuminates] it. The Lamb is its light." There will be no night there for it will be one great eternal day.

What is your idea of what it is going to be like in the new world? What will the activities be like? Will people just be sitting on clouds and playing harps?

God has spent 6,000 years preparing the great plan of redemption, the cleansing of mankind's sin, and a plan for spiritual growth. This growth involves the Holy Spirit and His leading and guidance. It also involves maturity and perfection. God has used the whole of the 6,000 years to complete His plan. He has been building a church and preparing a bride.

Then He has given 1,000 years to show what it is like to live in a world where there are no sin or sinners, and no devil. It is a time of peace and safety—a time where the Lord Jesus Christ rules and reigns. It is a time of no sickness or death.

Now there is a new heaven and a new earth to be inhabited. According to Revelation 21, there is a great city, the heavenly Jerusalem. According to verses three and four, God will dwell with His people, and He will be their God. In verse four, there will be no more tears. Chapter 21 speaks of a pure river of life that comes from the throne of God and the Lamb. We do not fully know what life will be like, but are sure that we will not just be sitting around doing nothing. God has not worked these thousands of years, building a church, preparing a church and a bride, and then preparing a new earth and heaven to have it merely end there.

CHAPTER 8

Heaven

HEAVEN AND HELL are real places—places prepared by the great Creator Himself. What does the Bible say about heaven? First of all, it is the place where God dwells. Moses, as part of the Law recorded in the book of Deuteronomy, said, "Look down from your holy habitation, from heaven, and bless your people Israel" (Deut. 26:15). Part of Solomon's prayer in 1 Kings 8:30 reads, "And may You hear the supplication of Your servant and of Your people Israel, when they pray toward this place. Hear in heaven Your dwelling place; and when You hear, forgive." The prayer that we call "The Lord's Prayer," the one that Jesus taught His disciples, as well as us, to pray, begins, "Our Father which art in heaven" (Matthew 6: 9 KJV). Stephen, just before he was martyred, gave a great message to the people. Part of that message was, "The Most High does not dwell in temples made with hands, as the prophet says, 'Heaven is my throne'" (Acts 7:48-49).

How long has heaven existed? That we really don't know, for it existed long before the creation of this world.

49

It goes back to the eternities before time began. Lucifer, now known as the devil or Satan, was cast out of heaven before creation because of his rebellion. Heaven is a place created by God. Though it has existed for a long time, it is not eternal. It will be replaced.

It is described as the place or home where the righteous dead go when they die. In part of the Sermon on the Mount, Jesus instructed us, "Do not lay up for yourselves treasures on earth, where moth and rust destroy, and where thieves break in and steal. For where your treasure is, there your heart will be also" (Matt. 6:19-21). The apostle John, while cast away on the Island of Patmos, described the things revealed to him. He said in Revelation 7:9-10, "After these things I looked, and behold, a great multitude which no one could number, of all nations, tribes, peoples, and tongues, standing before the throne and before the Lamb, clothed with white robes, with palm branches in their hands, and crying out with a loud voice, saying, 'Salvation belongs to our God who sits on the throne, and to the Lamb!'" Heaven is the place that Jesus spoke of when He said, "I go to prepare a place for you" (John 14:2). This place, by the way, is described in various ways in different translations. In the *King James* and the *New King James* versions, it is translated "mansions." In the *New International Version* and the *Goodspeed* Bible it is "many rooms." The *20th Century New Testament* renders it "dwellings." In the *Living Bible* it is "many homes." It is "many abodes" in Moffat's translation. It has been said, "Heaven is a prepared place for a prepared people."

There are angels in heaven, multitudes of them. John saw them. And he said, "The number of them was ten thousand times ten thousand, and thousands of thousands." He heard them, saying with loud voices, "Worthy is the Lamb who was slain, to receive power and riches and wisdom, and strength and honor and glory and blessing" (Revelation 5:11-12).

As mentioned, heaven is the place where the righteous dead go: "To be absent from the body is to be present with the Lord" (2 Corinthians 5:8). The thief on the cross, the one that wanted to be remembered by Jesus, was told by the Savior, "Today you will be with Me in Paradise" (Luke 23:43). Paradise is another word describing heaven. Paradise is also the place that Paul was caught up to, and where he heard words that he could not repeat or utter (2 Corinthians 12:4). In Revelation 2:7 it is also a place promised to those who overcome.

Heaven is absolutely a beautiful and wonderful place—a place where one would certainly long to be. Today all those who have left this earth to dwell there are in spirit forms. In death the spirit goes back to God because, "The body without the spirit is dead" (James 2:26.) The spirit is the real person, the part of you that will never die. The real part of you that will spend eternity some place. For the righteous—the godly—it will be with the Lord. Today that place is in heaven. These spiritual beings will soon be leaving heaven. They will depart from and vacate this glorious place. Their spirits will be reconciled to a body, an eternal body, a body that will never be sick or die again. They will be joined together with those who are alive at the time, those who will be changed, in a moment, in the twinkling of an eye. Together they will dwell and reign with Christ for the 1,000 years.

Angels are spirit beings that do not have bodies. Yet they can take on a bodily form to make an appearance here on earth. What kind of a body is that? Some have assumed that those who die, and whose spirits go to heaven, will receive some kind of temporary body, but we do not see that in

Scripture. It would appear that there are only four actual bodies in heaven: Enoch, Moses, Elijah, and Jesus.

In Genesis 5:24 we read that, "Enoch walked with God, and was not, for God took him." The explanation is given in Hebrews 11:5, "By faith Enoch was taken away so that he did not see death, and was not found because God had taken him." *King James* translates it, "Enoch was translated."

Concerning Moses, the book of Deuteronomy records the fact that Moses died in the land of Moab and the Lord buried him there. No one knows where his grave is. (See Deuteronomy 34:5-6.) Since when is God in the burial business? The little book of Jude informs us that there was a dispute over Moses' body. The dispute was between the devil and Michael the archangel. Michael did not dare bring a reviling accusation against Satan, but said, "The Lord rebuke you!" (Jude, verse 9). Now who do you think won that argument? We know that Moses appeared on the Mount of Transfiguration. He is also one of the two witnesses who will appear during the tribulation period.

In 2 Kings 2:11 we learn that Elijah went up into heaven in a whirlwind and a chariot of fire. He also appeared on the Mount of Transfiguration with Moses, and is the other witness during the time of tribulation.

Jesus, of course, died on the cross for our sins, was buried, and rose again the third day. Later He ascended back into heaven in clouds of glory, and is seated at the right hand of majesty today. These four, then, are in heaven in actual bodies.

But something happens at the end of the 1,000 years. There will be a new heaven, and a new earth. Revelation chapters 21 and 22 relate to us descriptions of this. The first heaven (or the heaven that has always been) will pass away, as will the earth. Why would God destroy heaven and earth? It has been suggested that He will do so because sin has tainted both places. Sin first entered into heaven when Lucifer, in his pride and arrogance, rebelled against God. Satan introduced that sin to earth through Adam and Eve.

From the descriptions in Revelation 21 and 22, there will be no more tears, death, sorrow, or crying. Everything is made new. There will be no night there. It will be one great eternal day. The light comes from the glory of God and the Lamb. There is a pure river of the water of life flowing from the throne. This is a perfect world, inhabited by a perfect people, ruled by a perfect God. Time will be no more. *This* is the eternal dwelling place for those who love God, for those who serve Him. (See again the end of chapter 7, "The Millennium.")

"Amazing Grace," one of the favorite hymns for many was written by a redeemed slave trader. The last verse says, "When we've been there ten thousand years, bright shining as the sun, we've no less days to sing God's praise than when we first begun." I suppose most of us thought that was up in heaven. Well, heaven's days are numbered, and so is the millennium, or a 1,000-year period. With the new heaven and the new earth, time has now come to an end. Since time will be no more, we will never know when 10,000 years have come and gone! It is one great eternal day!

What will it be like on a new earth? We really have no idea. We can only guess. God has brought about creation and mankind. He has spent six thousand years developing redemption, the creation of a church, and a bride. Then He spends 1,000 years showing what life on earth could be like without sin and the devil. Then He creates a new heaven and a new earth. Whenever God does a new thing, it is always an improvement or better than before. We have seen each thing God has done as something better, so now a new heaven and a new earth will be the very best, and it will be eternal.

What is the new earth like? Is it like this present earth? Much of this present earth is made up of oceans. In the new earth there will be no more sea (see Revelation 21:1). John, in this chapter, saw a city, the New Jerusalem, coming down out of heaven. He heard a loud voice out of heaven, saying, "Behold the tabernacle of God is with men, and He will dwell with them, and they shall be His people" (Revelation 21:2-3).

This city is described as a spectacular and glorious place. Many have looked upon this place as being heaven, but it is surely not the present heaven, and here it is called the New Jerusalem. Made up of many precious stones and jewels, the city is foursquare, its length, breadth, and height are all equal, with walls of jasper and throughout the place, gold as transparent as glass. The gates are of pearl, and the streets are of pure gold. Think of it, gold used as paving material!

The city has no temple, for the Father and the Son—the Lord God Almighty and the Lamb—are its temple. They are also the light of the city, so there is no need of the sun. The last verse of Revelation chapter 21 reveals that it is only for those, "Who are written in the Lamb's Book of Life."

John saw this city descending from heaven. Does it remain there, hovering over the earth? I hardly think so. If it descends to the earth, then it is on the earth. If this is where God will now dwell, for what reason is there a new heaven? If the New Jerusalem and the new heaven are the same, is this heaven on earth?

We actually know very little about what the new heaven and new earth will be like. There are only little glimpses of what God has revealed in these few passages of Scripture. After God created man, He came down to the garden to commune and fellowship with Adam. God had told Adam and Eve to be fruitful and multiply. If they had not sinned, and the number of people had multiplied, would God have continued to do this? Now this holy city, the New Jerusalem, is on the new earth, populated by redeemed and glorified saints. "Behold the tabernacle of God is with men, and He will dwell with them, and they shall be His people. God Himself will be with them, and be their God. And God will wipe every tear from their eyes; there shall be no more death, nor sorrow, nor crying. There shall be no more pain, for the former things are passed away" (Revelation 21:3-4). Is this, maybe, what God had in mind before sin came?

There are some things that puzzle this writer. It appears that there is no eating in heaven (the present one), but we will eat in the new earth. Scripture teaches that the life of the flesh is in the blood. We eat and digest food that enters the blood stream to feed the body, or the flesh. Blood is corruptible, therefore, flesh and blood cannot inherit the kingdom of God (1 Corinthians 15:50). So we are to be changed, in a moment, in the twinkling of an eye, and this corruption will take on incorruption, this mortal will take on immortality. In this new, glorified body, what is the need of food? Will it be digested? After the resurrection, Jesus, in His resurrected body, ate at least twice. When He appeared to them in an upper room, the doors being shut, He asked, "Do you have anything to eat?" They gave Him a piece of fish. Again, when He met the disciples in Galilee and prepared breakfast for them. This is just one of the little puzzles that baffle this writer. But it will all be revealed to us at that time. We have so much to learn!

Many other questions also arise. If the new earth is about the same size as the old, what will be the method of travel? In the present earth, the city of Jerusalem was the place designated for Israel to go to for various feasts and observances. Where will the New Jerusalem be located, perhaps in the same place? So how will we travel? Some have suggested we will travel as Philip did after baptizing the Ethiopian in water.

Surely, there is a lot to learn and experience about the new heaven and the new earth. Paul writes in 1 Corinthians 2:9, "Eye has not seen, nor ear heard, nor have entered into the heart of man the things which God has prepared for those who love Him." In the very next verse he says, "But God has revealed them to us through His Spirit." It is true that revelation has come to some by this means, and some (Paul) have been caught up to heaven. Yet the fullness and the greatness, beauty and splendor is yet to be seen by most of us. We can be assured that what God has prepared for His people will be glorious and wonderful, the culmination of all He has done through the ages.

CHAPTER 9

The Calendar

THIS LAST CHAPTER is somewhat different than our previous studies. It is not necessarily based specifically on what the Scriptures say, neither is it comparing scripture with scripture. There is definitely some speculation in the following thoughts, and the purpose is really just to cause one to think.

There is one fundamental question regarding the calendar. Where in the scheme of things are we today? Following our present day calendar it is basically impossible to try to fit in Bible prophecy. Just exactly where are we in the light of the things we can understand from the Word of God? There have been (and there are) numerous calendars. There are Jewish, Babylonian, Greek, Muslim, Hindu, Chinese, Mexican or Aztec, American Indian, among others.

EARLY ROMAN CALENDAR

This calendar was devised by Romulus in 600 to 700 B.C. It had ten months and it began in the month of March. It had ten months, six were comprised of 30 days and four of 31 days, for a total of 304 days. The year ended in December, and they then had what they called a winter gap. The second king of Rome added January and February, adding 50 days, for a total of 354 days.

ROMAN REPUBLICAN CALENDAR

This calendar was brought about by the fifth king of Rome. It had only 355 days, ten-and-a-quarter days short of the tropical, or solar, year. Once every two years they added 27 or 28 days between February 23 and 24, and then they eliminated the last five days of February.

This was basically a lunar reckoning, and it became increasingly out of sync with the seasons as time passed. For example: About 50 B.C. the vernal equinox should have fallen late in March, instead it was eight weeks later on the Ides of May. It would have been necessary to add months, much as the Roman calendar needed to do.

JULIAN CALENDAR

About 50 B.C. (mid first-century B.C.) Julius Caesar asked an Alexandrian astronomer, Sosigenes, to revive the calendar. He abandoned the lunar calendar altogether. Months were now arranged on a seasonal basis, and a tropical (solar) year, the same as the Egyptian calendar. Its length was 365 ¼ days. It was too long; the tropical year is 365.242199 days. That's an error of 11 minutes, 14 seconds per year, or one-and-a-half days in two centuries, seven days in 1,000 years.

THE GREGORIAN CALENDAR

By the year 1545 the vernal equinox (used to determine Easter) had moved ten days. At the council of Trent (December 1545) Pope Paul III was authorized to correct the calendar. However, neither he nor his successors were able to do so. Many adjustments were necessary. Because Easter was the most important feast of the Christian church, its place in the calendar determined the rest of the church's feasts.

What we have today is basically the Gregorian calendar. It begins on January 1. The year 532 was adopted as the Greek Paschal period, making 1 A.D. as the first year of the calendar. In the sixth century it was believed that this was the year when Christ was born.

The Gregorian calendar was adopted slowly by various countries. France, Italy, Luxembourg, Portugal, and Spain adopted it in 1582. It was used by most German Catholic states, Belgium and Netherlands by 1584. It was gradually adopted in Switzerland from 1583 to 1812, Hungary in 1587, Denmark and the German Protestant states in 1699-1700. By Britain in 1752, Sweden in 1753, Japan in 1873, and in Egypt in 1875. Between 1912 and 1917 it was adopted by Albania, Bulgaria, and Yugoslavia. The Soviet Union adopted it in 1918, and Greece in 1923.[1]

It is from this calendar that we try to make a timetable to fit in Bible prophecies. How accurate is it, and does it begin in the right place or year? From this calendar, the birth of Christ would be in the first year, and His death on the cross would be the year 33.

```
0 ——————————————————————— 33 AD
Birth                       Cross
```

But that could actually be four years off. During the sixth century they started the calendar at the year they believed Christ was born, and called it 0. It is now believed that He was born before that time. A number of years for His birth have been presented, but 4 B.C. seems to make the most sense. In the 70 week prophecy in Daniel 9, the period of time from the commandment given to restore Jerusalem unto the coming of the Messiah was to be 69 weeks, or 483 years. That would make the year 26 A.D. the time that Jesus was baptized and the Holy Spirit came upon Him. Messiah and Christ are the same words, the first is Hebrew, the other Greek, and both mean the "Anointed One." Thus the adjustment would be:

4BC ————————————— 29 AD
Birth   Cross

These adjustments would make the end of 2,000 years to be 1996, but nothing happened in that year, nor did it happen in the year 2000. *But, wait just a minute!* Should this dispensation even start at Jesus' birth? We have two great periods in Bible history. They are LAW and GRACE.

At the time of the birth of Christ, they were under the LAW. When He was growing up, they were under LAW. When He began His ministry at the age of 30, and ministered for three-and-a-half years, they were still under LAW.

So when did grace begin? *At the cross!* When was the church born? Fifty days later at Pentecost! What was the year? *Probably 29 A.D.* So if we begin the dispensation of grace at the year of the crucifixion and birth of the church, it would start at the year 29, now numbered one, and end after 2,000 years. To fit this into our present calendar, if we add the year 29 to 2000, we should get the year when this dispensation ends. That would be the year 2029. If we

60

subtract the year we are in, we would get the number of years remaining.

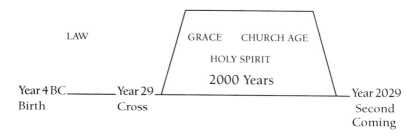

LAW

GRACE   CHURCH AGE

HOLY SPIRIT

2000 Years

Year 4 BC ———— Year 29 ———————————————— Year 2029
Birth   Cross   Second
                                                  Coming

What will the last days be like? In Matthew 24:3-14 we read about wars and rumors of wars, nation against nation. There are famines and pestilence and earthquakes in a variety of places. The Bible states that these are but the beginning of sorrows. There is persecution and hatred of Christians by all nations. There is betrayal and false prophets and lawless ones. In 2 Thessalonians 2:8,9 the antichrist is called the lawless one. Also in that chapter is mentioned the "mystery of lawlessness."

In 2 Timothy 3:1-5, we are informed that in the last days perilous times will come. Men will be lovers of themselves. They will be covetous, boasters, proud, blasphemers, disobedient to parents, unthankful and unholy. They will be without natural affection, will be trucebreakers, incontinent, fierce, and despisers of those that are good. They will also be traitors, heady, high-minded, and lovers of pleasure more than lovers of God. They will have a form of godliness, but will deny its power. (KJV)

In Luke 17:22-36, Jesus said it would be like the days of Noah and like the days of Sodom. During this time period, we also have the woman (church) going into the wilderness, a man ruling over all tribes, tongues, and nations, which would include the United States. All of this would have to happen in the few remaining years of this dispensation. Some might say, "Are you setting dates?" *Absolutely not!* These are suggestions—things to make one think.

The Bible says that no man knows the day or the hour, only the Father in heaven knows. We are assuming that the age or dispensation is 2,000 years. Although we believe it is, we cannot be certain. Also, we do not know the calendar that God uses, or even if He uses a calendar. Does He accept or follow the Jewish calendar? Does He accept or approve of our present calendar? Does His calendar start with the beginning of time and go right through to the end, ignoring any and all other calendars? If this is the case, just when does time begin? We are told in Matthew 24:22 that, "Unless those days were shortened, no flesh would be saved; but for the elect's sake those days will be shortened." What about that? What does it mean? It would really be arrogant to assume you can predict the exact date, year, or time. The Bible simply says, "Be ready!"

The purpose of the thoughts or studies in this chapter, as mentioned previously, is to cause one to think. Where are we? Are we close to the end of the age, and if so, just how close? There is one thing that is very certain; it is truly the time to seek the Lord and to pray. He has revival for the church, a purifying and cleansing revival that prepares her to be the church described as being without spot or wrinkle. Thinking of where we are, or might be, should cause every believer to seek God as never before. We need His presence and power to be able to stand in the end time. We need a vision, "For without a vision the people perish." We need revival!

God has been preparing for this great final event since before the actual beginning of time. This is the finality, the climax, of what He has been building. It is the revelation of His finished product, His masterpiece. "To those who eagerly wait for Him, He will appear a second time, apart from sin, for salvation" (Hebrews 9:28).

If God has been working on a plan for many thousands of years, what must the future be like? Are we just going to heaven to sit on a cloud and play a harp? Are we going merely to be among a number, like the angels, that continue to praise and magnify the Lord? (Although that would be a wonderful thing!) There will be a new heaven and a new earth, and for the first time, there will be a perfect government. If God has been making preparations for this great city (which is more like a nation), how wonderful and magnificent it will be. Don't miss it!

AN ADDED NOTE

This study on the calendar was first presented more than a year before the last presidential election. At that time, we did not know who would be the next president, but based on changes in our country over the past few years, I made the statement, "America, as we have known it, will never be the same." This was based on a number of things. One, with the great number of immigrants from other countries, voting patterns are changing. Also, the values of the great number of young people coming to voting age are changing. Then, with the knowledge that the United States will be among the nations that serve a world dictator, the antichrist, it was easy to see that great change was coming. Today, this writer is more convinced of this fact than ever before.

J. Lee Grady, editor of *Charisma*, recently wrote, "Change is hitting America between the eyes. Everything that can be shaken is being shaken—from banks and insurance companies to car manufacturers and media empires.

Trusted brands, including Chrysler and United Airlines, may go out of business within months. Newspapers are laying off employees in droves as readers go digital. What we are experiencing today is more than an economic recession. The upheaval is affecting us politically, socially, technologically, and spiritually. It feels as if God has pushed a giant red reset button in heaven. Change is being forced upon us."[2]

Conclusion

IT HAS BEEN the purpose of these studies to try to see just what the Bible says, and then to test teachings or doctrines based on that. Our main study has been to see what it says about eschatology, the end, or last time events. It is hoped that one may not only know what it is they believe, but *why* they believe it. We can learn by memory what a teaching is, and can repeat it. A parrot and a tape recorder can do the very same thing. Some churches have catechism classes for children, and at a certain age, they are tested during confirmation on what they have learned. However, while they may know the doctrine, they do not really understand it.

Repeating what was said in the introduction, our redemption and salvation is not based upon our beliefs concerning eschatology. It is based on the redemption purchased by our Savior when He shed his blood on the cross and when He died for our sins.

George E. Ladd, in his book, *The Blessed Hope,* writes, "Neither pretribulationism nor postribulationism should be made a ground of fellowship, a test of orthodoxy, or a necessary element in Christian doctrine. There should be liberty and charity toward both views."[1]

Our fellowship is based on our belief in Christ as our Savior, and a Christian experience that has produced a new life. Old things have passed away. It is a belief in a separated life and Bible holiness, "Without which no one will see the Lord" (Hebrews 12:14).

We are part of the family of God, a family that is made up of blood-washed saints. We are part of a body, the body of Christ. We are brothers and sisters, and Christ is our Elder Brother. His Father is our Father, and we are one in Him. We all worship Him together, and all praise and honor goes to Him.

There are teachings that are contrary to the basics of salvation and the gospel. Paul, in Galatians 1, speaks of those bringing in what he called, "another Gospel." He said, "Let them be accursed." This can be a difference that we stand against and which we oppose. There is no fellowship with such. Also, "Have no fellowship with the unfruitful works of darkness" (Eph. 5:11). And again, "But we commend, you brethren, in the name of our Lord Jesus Christ, that you withdraw from every brother who walks disorderly and not according to the tradition which he received from us" (2 Thess. 3:6). These are different issues on which there can be no compromise. However, our differences in eschatology should not hinder our fellowship with one another.

When it comes to teaching, or our interpretation of Bible references with regard to future events (eschatology), we may disagree, but we should never be disagreeable. As Abraham said to his nephew, Lot, "We are brethren." There should be love for one another in the body of Christ. We can have discussions concerning our beliefs, but should not be involved in great arguments. Jesus said, "By this all will know that you are my disciples, if you have love for one another" (John 13:35).

There is one thing all believers should agree on, that is, Jesus *is* coming back again! The Bible clearly reveals this great fact to us. It is an absolute Bible truth.

- John 14:3: "And if I go and prepare a place for you, *I will come again* and receive you to myself, that where I am, there you may be also" (emphasis mine).
- Hebrews 9:28: "So Christ was offered once to bear the sins of many. To those who eagerly wait for Him *He will appear a second time*, apart from sin, for salvation" (emphasis mine).
- Philippians 3:20: "For our citizenship is in heaven, *from which we eagerly wait for the savior, the Lord Jesus Christ*" (emphasis mine).
- Titus 2:13: "Looking for the blessed hope and *glorious appearing of our great God and Savior Jesus Christ.*" Acts 1:11: "This same Jesus, who was taken up from you into heaven, *will so come in like manner* as you saw Him go into heaven" (emphasis mine).

The second coming of Christ is said to be mentioned 318 times in the New Testament, which is an average of once in every 25 verses.

The Second Coming is the one great event for which we all should be preparing. Jesus gave a number of teachings, sometime in parables, emphasizing the need for readiness for the coming king. "Therefore, you also be ready, for the Son of Man is coming at an hour you do not expect" (Matt. 24:44).

God is still on His throne, He is still in charge and in control. It will all happen and take place just the way He desires. He has given us quite a number of clues in His Word, but there will probably be a few surprises for all of us as it all happens. Hindsight is so much easier than foresight. The prophecies with regard to the Messiah's birth were all there in the Old Testament, but the Messiah did not come in the way the people were expecting, and consequently they rejected Him

In the meeting of the colonists just before the Declaration of Independence, one of the founding fathers said, "We must all hang together, or we will hang separately." Those of the body of Christ, the blood-washed saints, need to "hang together" as we enter into what we believe are the times of the end. We definitely need one another in fellowship and in sincere worship as never before. He *is* coming back again, and truly this is our *blessed hope.*

A PREPARED PLACE

Don't be troubled, in life's great struggle,
For in God you do believe.
Believe also in the Son, He's the only One,
The Person all must receive.
To Father's house He'll go, He wants you to know,
There are many dwelling places there.
He will prepare you a place, provided by His grace,
And then life with Him you will share.
He's returning again, to take you with Him,
There to spend eternity.
The place you know, and the way you know,
So it's really a certainty.
But then one says, "no, we really don't know,
So how can we know the way?"
"The answer is plain," He went on to explain,
"It's as clear as the light of day.
The way is Me, so why can't you see,
In Me is the life and truth also.
The Father receives none, no not one,
Unless through Me they go."
Renus R. Cabe
Based on John 14:1-6

Endnotes

Chapter 1: The Rapture

1 George E. Ladd, *The Blessed Hope*, p. 71.
2. ibid., p. 73.
3. Charles Larkin, *Dispensational Truth*, 1918, 1920.
4. George E. Ladd, *The Blessed Hope*, p. 71.

Chapter 2: The Woman in Revelation 12

1. Kevin Conner, *The Book of Revelation*, p. 365, 2001.
2. W .W. Patterson, *Treasures from the Book of Daniel and the Book of Revelation*, p. 40.
3. G. Campbell Morgan, *The Parables and Metaphors of our Lord*.

Chapter 3: Revival

1. Charles Finney, *Revivals of Religion*.
2. ibid.

Chapter 4: The Marriage of the Lamb

1. Edward T. Hiscox, *Star Book for Ministers*, p. 213.
2. *The International Standard Bible Encyclopedia*, Vol. III, p. 1999.
3. W.H. Offiler, *God and His Bible, or the Harmonies of Divine Revelation*, p. 48.
4. ibid, p. 132.

Chapter 5: Daniel's Seventieth Week

1. W.W. Patterson, *Bible Treasures from Daniel*, p. 25.

Chapter 9: The Calendar

1. The information concerning calendar history was gleaned from, *The Encyclopedia Britannica*, Vol 2, p. 740; Vol 15, p. 447.
2. J. Lee Grady, *Charisma*, p. 6, June, 2009.

Conclusion

1. George E. Ladd, *The Blessed Hope*, p. 167.

Bibliography

Conner, Kevin, *The Book of Revelation,* KJC Publications, 2001. Australia.

Encyclopedia Britannica, Volume #2, Volume #15, 15th Edition. Chicago, IL

Finney, Charles G., *Revivals Of Religion,* CBN University Press. 1978. Virginia Beach, VA

Grady, J. Lee, *Charisma* magazine, June, 2009. Strang Media, Lake Mary, FL 32746

Hiscox, Edward T., *The Star Book for Ministers,* , The Judson Press. Philadelphia, PA.

Ladd, George E., *The Blessed Hope* Wm. B. Eerdmans Publishing Company. Grand Rapids, MI

Larkin, Clarence, *Dispensational Truth,* 1918, 1926. Philadelphia. PA

Morgan, G. Campbell, *The Parables and Metaphors Of Our Lord*, Marshal Morgan and Scott, Ltd. 1940

Offiler, W.H., *God and His Bible, or Harmonies of Divine Revelation*. Seattle, WA.

Patterson, W. W., *Bible Treasures from the Book of Daniel and the Book of Revelation*. 1973

The International Standard Bible Encyclopedia, Wm. B. Eerdmans Publishing Co. Grand Rapids, MI.

LaVergne, TN USA
02 November 2010
203247LV00003B/37/P